"Oh My Heck!"

A pretty, great cartoon book

by Pat Bagley

Signature Books
Salt Lake City
1988

for Wendy

and in memory of
Gregg Alvord

Book design by Connie Disney

LIBRARY OF CONGRESS CATALOGING-IN-PUBLICATION DATA
Bagley, Pat, 1956–
    Oh my heck! / Pat Bagley
        p.   cm.
    ISBN 0-941214-68-0
    I. Title
PN6162.B26 1988
41.5'973–dc19

88-30865
CIP

"I cannot easily conceive of anything more cozy than the night in Salt Lake which we spent in a Gentile den, smoking pipes and listening to tales of how. . .heedless people often come to Utah and make remarks about Brigham, or polygamy, or some other sacred matter, and the very next morning at daylight such parties are sure to be found lying up some back alley, contentedly waiting for the hearse. . ."

—Mark Twain, *Roughing It*

pretty great leisure

"I think it needs a comma."

"Image Problem? What image problem?"

"We send out pairs of clean-cut young men and women into the world to go door to door bearing witness to the vacation potential of our state. What a novel idea!"

Utah Boosters in Hell

"Don't give them anything. . . .
Do you want more of their kind coming here?"

"They're in the bushes again, LaVar...Turn the hose on them."

"Say, ain't that the tourist feller who thought Nutcracker was a 'cute' name for a horse?"

"'A nice secluded spot,' you said...'Our own private paradise,' you said...
'A million miles from anyone,' you said..."

"No, Honey. It's only called Goblin Valley..."

"Your father is wrestling with the elements to provide sustenance for his family. In the meantime, would you like a tuna sandwich?"

pretty, great politics

"Then it's agreed: Muffy hijacks all the hairspray coming into the state;
George eliminates all the easy listening systems; and Carl blacks out the BYU/U of U game.
Comrades, by this time tommorow Utah will be plunged into anarchy!"

"We chose Utah because this is the only place in America
where we could enjoy all the privileges of living back home."

FIRST IT WAS FLOODING, NOW IT'S THE GREENHOUSE EFFECT... GOT ANY IDEAS?
NARM
WHIRRRRRR
ENVIRO-MASTER
AIR CONDITIONING
WALKER

"Senator Hatch must have popped in..."

"...an' let's eliminate taxes on necessities—like four-wheelers, huntin' rifles an' ammo, snowmobiles..."

"Merrill, I think we found something you can win."

"Good work, men.
Lord knows what havoc those half-dozen Blue Mouse patrons might have wreaked
had they been allowed to finish watching that dirty artsy movie."

"Ali, it's really a sweet gesture...Golly, I'm really touched."

"Overcrowding and the quality of education aren't the issues here, Miss Stotesberry. The real issue is–are you now or have you ever been a secular humanist?"

"Ladies, our goal is to take sex out of the schools and put it back in the gutter—where it belongs."

Utah Pillage & Loot

"Mrs. Garn, we suspect your husband is an escapee
from the space cadet academy on tri-alpha-epsom."

A pretty, great religion.

"You know what this means—
we've got to jiggle two million lights till we find which one is loose."

"All those in favor of sustaining me—Verlin Parley Orrin Hyrum—
as prophet, seer, and revenging angel of the First Born Church of the Last Days,
please manifest it by the usual sign."

"Sister Finchley, I'm tired of these newspaper articles accusing the church of calling all the shots in Utah... Have the state legislature pass a resolution denying it."

"So in between this life and our final reward we go to a place called *Saint George*."

"Brother Smith, one does not shout 'Get Down'
in the middle of the 'Hallelujah Chorus.'"

" 'We'll crush your vile little business. We'll destroy your poor excuse of a company. We'll drive you to your corporate knees. Cordially, your brother in the gospel.' "

A pretty, great social scene.

"But I can't marry him. He smokes."

"So when I'm not climbing Everest or helping underprivileged children,
I'm working on a cure for cancer. . .Wanna get naked?"

"Ya know, Honey, it doesn't get any better than this."

pretty, great sports

"Hurry! Over here! Bring this man his Finisher's T-shirt!"

"What do you say we finish this round and then take in a couple of sessions
at the nineteenth?"

"My name is Bobby, but you all can call me Mr. Thurgood."

"Switching the trail sign was a terrific idea.
I just love watching their goofy expressions."

"Give them a '10' on the Groveling Portion of the selection process."

"What's he mean by 'horizontally tall'?"

"Lissen up men. Here's our new game plan for beating BYU."

"...and Sheide begat Nielsen, and Nielsen begat Wilson, and Wilson begat McMahon, and McMahon begat Young, and Young begat Bosco..."

"Yeah, we got a real good deal on some old boosters from Morton Thiokol."

A pretty, great past.

"This Lake Bonneville Pumping Project is a mammoth waste, if you ask me."

"I think I've cracked it:
'Ambitious, bright, sensitive warrior, 28, seeks long-term relationship
with attractive member of opposite sex...'"

"Why should I care if you dig in my tribal burial grounds?"

"Damn!"

"All I know is that they were cold-blooded, had brains the size of a peanut, and that a few of them can still be found in the state legislature."

A pretty, special state.

"...and you say you have proof that LDS church officials write acid-rock music...
uh huh...and that they operate a white slavery ring out of the Eagle Gate Apartment
...uh huh...and that they grow psychedelic mushrooms in the temple..."

"I happen to know for a fact that the man who designed this house
is also responsible for some of the country's most beautiful Motel Sixes."

"I'm Rod Decker. My guests tonight are
the Ladies of Midvale Prince of Darkness Witches' Coven and Male Emasculation Society
who are eager to show that they're just regular folks."

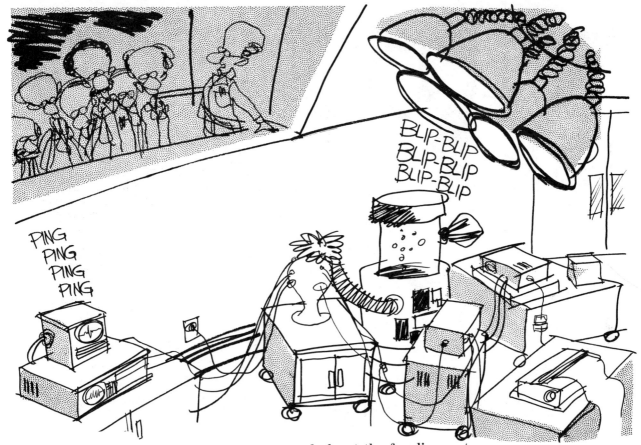

"We were concerned about the funding cuts,
but I'm happy to report our Jarvik-7 artifical hairpiece is a success."

"If this is the Lord's University,
then I guess that makes us the Lord's Part-Time Cafeteria Help."

"Pat, I'd like to buy a Salamander Letter."

"What do you mean it's 'inappropriate?'"

"So what is it today, Mark?
The beginning of another ice age or catastrophic warming due to the Greenhouse Effect?"

"I assure you, sir. There is nothing wrong with the cut of the suit.
Have you considered corrective surgery?"

"About the article you submitted–
the writing is pretentious, the tone is arrogant, and the subject matter is presumptuous.
I loved it."

THE GREAT PYRAMIDS OF EGYPT

THE GREAT PYRAMIDS OF UTAH

"And remember that this isn't just any run-of-the-mill, garden variety white stuff—
this is the Greatest Snow on Earth."

The "This is the Place" Monument

The "I Think I'll Take that Job in San Diego" Monument

"You drag me halfway across the country to see some half-rate, special effects?"